Stranger Paths

The Magic in The Madness

Poetry Collection

By R.J. Zarkani

Stranger Paths
Part I

Of Childhood & War

Part I contains over thirty short poems shining a light on the untold truths of war. Between living under Saddam Hussein's rule and witnessing the start of The Iraq War, young Raghad had an interesting life story that had to be told. The author wishes to share her story through poetry in hopes to inspire the survivor in you, the reader.

Key players in Part I: the memories of her childhood village and the wild dogs that lived there; the Iraq war as it began and the consequences after; and lastly, the hope that inspired the author to have a unique perspective on life.

My Title

The child that stood on tip toes

Trying to see the men outside

Through bullet holes I watched

Much too excited for change

"It will be beautiful, like America... like you see on
TV." One solider promised me

That was back in 2003

When ISIS was a nightmare yet to form

When angels wore uniforms

When enemies were clear to see

When I did not know the difference between you and
me

But now my skin gives me a label I did not earn

Not a "Doctor"

"Woman"

"Rich" nor "Poor"

I wear a title that I cannot for the life of me shed

But that is a thing I dare not regret

The Test

I wondered who he was

As I passed his broken car

As I witnessed his blood freed from his body

And the army sounding from afar

Was he a bomber, choosing to die?

Was he a fool that did not check his car?

Then I ran

Late for my midterm exam

...

And 'til this day, I can't remember for the life of me
if I passed the test

A Memory

Fireworks

Bright

Making a day out of night

13-years-old

I did not mind

Invade or liberate

That must be a freedom sound

Adults crying

Dad asking me to get inside

But I wanted to see it

I no longer wanted to hide

So I stood on the rooftop

Witnessing history being made

History from a Child's Point of View

She reveals pieces of herself, every now and then

On reflective surfaces when light is not too dim

Sun shines through the shattered window...

That window that could not withstand the blow

And the shaking of the ground

...

It was **not** a nightmare

It was her life

...

Where explosions mask cries

There she stood, praying to die

She asked for the meaning of life

Her town seemed like a soldier's toy

In Iraq I buried that girl

SHE WAS ME

Letter to Baghdad

She swallowed the smoke and the bombs away

She exploded turning to shards that day

Baghdad I'm sorry for the burden you had to carry

Souls exploding and imploding that you bury

They don't know the beauty that you used to be

The singing and dancing in your streets

The way the ground felt so safe and secure

Baghdad, I don't know you anymore

Saddam Hussein

His picture hung

On every classroom wall

We sung him songs

Every day in our old school hall

Children, we were

They hid the truth

Until the day

He was captured by the troops

I thought him a hero

Or something close

Then they told us what hid beneath those cloaks

The uncle I did not know I had

The others hidden from sight

Their stories shed a different light

The man children were told to worship

Was the evil of their land

The confusion of a child

The story I could not understand

Truth Told

A memory that's not yet old

Her, laying on my dorm room bed

Fever filling her head

Gun shots sounding closer and closer

Baghdad, what have we done?

I kiss her forehead, cover her with my blankets

Sister, what have we done?

I told her I must step outside

But she couldn't hear

The small glass window was near

And it was threatening to break

Everyone was screaming

I wished I'd been dreaming

But I thought I had to say my goodbyes

...

Sister we've come so far

This truth had to be told

Before our story got too old

And everyone forgot we existed

Have You Seen God

I think I have

Somewhere north of Al-Kut south of Baghdad

He stopped by a broken house

A broken man was put back together

Hope

That's all he needed

To withstand the weather

. . .

Have you seen God

Did you look

As you passed by the weary soul

The closed door

The broken bridge

Did you look

Or did you just search for a detour

. . .

He was there

He is here

As we look for him in the clouds

He stands near

Foot prints that we fail to follow

Too foreign for us to understand

So we refuse to take his hand

Rooftops

Flat rooftops

Candles in my hands

Listening to counting crows

Baghdad, you don't look like Baltimore

Baghdad, I don't know you anymore

But I'm still here

On rooftops

Counting buildings

As they disappear

Hero?

He was her hero…he was her knight

The teachers preached about his loving heart

A loving president and a loving man

His name was Saddam

She believed that he was as kind as God; sometimes
she thought he was a God

Warm hearted and kind to all

He was her own Santa Clause

But at 13 years of age, her hero was caged

He was no longer magnificent or godly

He was found in a hole underground

Then he was hung like pirates used to be hung

The news declared him as a villain, a runaway and a
murderer

She found out that her uncle disappeared because of
him, Saddam

She learned that her parents were too scared to tell
her the truth

And her teachers were too scared to teach what they
needed to

She did not know what to believe in anymore
She is me

Never Forget

I wish I can

But my skin and my color shows God's plan

I can never forget the wars you caused

The "Oh lookout, might be a terrorist" thoughts

Two buildings

And MILLIONS of casualties of war

One plane that began it all

Sorry

They poisoned the dogs in my street

They said I can no longer give them food to eat

But I'd always finish half of my plate

Save it for midnight

When it's much too late

Then I go running with the wild dogs

They poisoned the dogs in my street

And I still refuse to eat

The food on my plate

Boxes

Take me out of this box you made for me!

"You don't look like a terrorist" she says to me.

As I take a sip of my drink, I smile, for she thought
she complimented me

I get lost in the ignorance... or maybe it's innocence
that puts me in such a box

Should I change my name? Maybe dye my hair blond
just so you can relate to me?

The Wide-Eyed Girl

The wide eyes blinked

It was over

The war has engulfed the pond, the garden and the moon

It wasn't her choice

She smiled

Too young to worry, too old to cry

The wide eyes stared at a green leaf among the ruins

The birds might come back

She poured what's left of her water on what's left of a tree

The apples will grow!

Where My Roots Disappear

Here lies a dream

In papers drowned by ink

Things, even if you steal, you can never take

Land I forget, before I remember

Places where I used to belong

Earth that smelled much like

I

There I lay

And awake I see

There can be another me

Immigrant in this earth but free

My Sands

You might have thought me poor

Digging for hours in the dirt

Trying to find pieces of my childhood

Yeah...they might have thought me poor

Carrying pieces of sand, acting like they were jewels
in my hands...

See, they used to be my own

Earth and dirt to which I belonged

I find me poor these days

With toys already made

Play-Doh, I did not create

A screen play I did not write

This...none of this... is my own

It's their thoughts that I came to believe

You might see me looking for a diamond ring, for a
white car, to cover up how poor I feel

about what we are

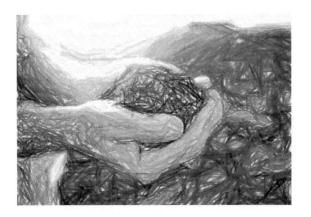

Mornings in Al-Kut

I remember when I was maybe eleven

I had to wake up as early as seven, rush to the
neighborhood baker

He made our street smell like heaven

The fresh bread gives me warmth on my morning
walk

And a lady sitting in the street

Selling something to eat

Breakfast routine that I love to remember

Memories of early December

She

She was a child

Happy with no cares

Explosions sounded close

But she had no fears

She was a child

No stress yet learned

And so, she saw fireworks

As her world burned

Memory of the War

The rumbling of the house

Soon after the explosion

I turn the radio up

And push it closer to her ear

She needs it more than I do

But as the radio dies

I can hear their cries

And I wonder

What did a 15-year-old do

To deserve this?

Imagine

I know this is a *black* and *white* battle

And *brown* is not in between

Maybe it is a color that your lens has not seen

But imagine for a moment or two

That it was you

Imagine being born to such a bad circumstance

That being caught in a boarder provides a better chance

Have you earned that ground you call home?

Or were you, like them, just born?

Hello My Old Self

I did not know

Where she went

Or where to go

To find that girl that glared through my mirror

Hello my old self

Where did you hide

Did this world rip you out from my insides

Did the glass prove too sharp

And life too dim

For me to ever see your innocent grin

?

Flowers

My flowers have no color

No roots

No earth to which they belong

My flowers are immigrants

Forgotten after hearing a cheerful song

You acted like you cared, for a moment

Then changed the channel

I wouldn't blame you

But **don't blame** my thorny flower

A Note She Wrote

Take them...those treasures I hide

Leave me with thoughts hidden deep inside

Leave me bare, naked, but content

Rob me of this life

You have my consent

Differences

The difference between you and me

Boils down to geography

I was born somewhere far beyond your sea

And so, you see me differently

...

The difference between a citizen and a refugee

Is just

Another disaster of this world I see

Miles define who we are and who we can be

...

If you weren't born where you were

Who would you be?

Rain

Feet bare

Shoes were weighed down by mud

The wild dogs of my neighborhood escorting me
home

It was a day like no other

Rain in the desert

Streets Flooded

Is this what we all prayed for?

Flood to distract us from war

Optimistic View

I have witnessed a dictator's death due to his own
greed
I've witnessed a great war

I've made it across the world, safe

I have no doubt that God is stronger than man

So, relax, if you can

This is a life memory that you can later say

I witnessed that on this day

The Untold

Her name was difficult

From a land he's never seen

And her face was delicate

Unlike anything on T.V. screens

But her story was not a movie

It's one that has never been told

And she keeps quiet

Hoping the story will get old

And no other will be created

With such cruelty and pain

Still he wonders how to pronounce her name

2003 in History

They were barefooted

Running after the tanks

Men dressed the color of desert

Staring at the foreigner's hands

Children waving

Glorious day

When they believed what the soldiers had to say

Freedom I long to know

Freedom they told me so

Adapting

In a crack between two bricks

I left a message as I was taken away

And freed from the rooftops

I was allowed to visit the beach this May

Rain disturbed the strangers

But I was so happy to be free

And as time passed

I forgot the rooftops

And I was much like those strangers

Begging for sunshine

The Transformation

I WAS HERE

You scream

As their faces wrinkle with shock

I WAS

A dust in the air

A fly on the wall

A beautiful scent

A flower that grew tall

I was here through it all

And I have never left

Nor will I ever go

I am here body and soul

For we can never die

We merely transform

Survivor

I'm alive she said

But why? He wondered

I'm alive she said

But how? They wondered

But she never wondered

She knew

She will make it through

The Child Within

The child within smiles at the toys I see

The child within is happy to be me

Fascinated by the street lights and the sounds of the
sirens that she'd only heard on TV

She wished this for me

The child within got me as far as she could

And now she smiles

Watches my life unfold as it should

A Thanks to Earth

Immigrant, I thought I had left my home

Here to a new place where I did not belong

But as I saw the moon I did not feel so alone

Comforted by what I knew, I stared into space

The clouds looked familiar

And between the cracks of grey sky I found my place

The stars knew me, and the sun could relate

Then I understood

The earth is vast, and it does not discriminate

Part II

Of Positivity & Philosophy
A Spiritual Journey

This chapter holds poems that play with positivity to show the good in the bad and the choice of happiness. Philosophical thoughts come into play every now and then encouraging the reader to wonder about life, why are we here and how we came to be. Adam and Eve's story is a strong point of thought in the author's imagination. She hopes to inspire thought and happiness in her readers.

Future

A change in desire

Shifted the view

And now

I no longer fear you

Future

You are never to be realized

Lost between present and past

For tomorrow will always turn to today

Transmutation

They said he was a victim

Of strangers and the system

Of things no one could control

But he chose to be an inspiration

Used his challenge as motivation

And proved it to them all

Now he guides the people

Teaching them of what they're able

Expanding boxes and making them few

This hero is no stranger

This hero could easily be YOU

Why He Stands

They cut his chains

Without asking

They cut his chains

Without telling

Him

Fight

You fight because

If you survive

You will have a story

Larger than life

Colors

I am not black nor white

Somewhere in between

And grey is no color for a human being

Yet I feel

You

Her

Him

I feel what they can and cannot become

And I wonder if humans saw in black and white
lenses

Would it matter much to anyone

The colors we carry

?

Religions

Some are truths

Some are lies

Some are stories

Told too many times

Your Secret

You don't remember falling

But you must've fallen... reasons why you were born
crying

You forget what you've forgotten

You think they'll think you're insane

When you deny your new name

So, you shut out what you remember

A haze of a spirit entering a body

Energizing this entity

Your secret is safe

Even you can no longer tell

The truth from the myth

Awakening

You scream out and they forget why

You awake and start to cry

Oh this earth, I longed to view

Oh this earth, has room for but few

And I was chosen

And after the choice

I was frozen

By hearing my new voice

So, let me scream a moment or two

For soon I'll forget what I came here to do

...

Do you remember your purpose?

Hunt Party

There was a shift in consciousness

A change in view

The monster was a man

Holding a gun at you

You were the duck that landed

Trusting before you flew

Now you are back to your body

Not knowing what to do

Maybe I am the monster and the victim

Or just consciousness floating between bodies

Trying to find an answer

Of why

Must we kill to eat and live to die?

Strange Things

Let us fall

Although children we may no longer be

In this skin torn

Old

And wrinkly

We begin

Again, and again

Like the seeds falling from a tree

Birthed from death

Oh, what a strange thing to see

This drifting soul becoming me

The Key

She found the key!

But forgot to which door...

"I HAVE THE KEY!" She screamed, "Don't know
what for."

Gate after gate... trying to unlock a riddle

She tried to escape but she's stuck in the middle

Of man-made cages

Thought

There it goes

Hiding behind logic and what it knows

An idea that's not fully formed

The thought changes and grows

Quietly lurking in a corner of my brain

Not ready to scream out its name

Lost Opportunity

I rejected it before I asked why it cannot be

An idea

A thought

That did not agree with me

I rejected it because it was different than what I have
believed

And so, a great idea was never conceived

Unknown

How did the sculptor know

There's a woman hidden in the stone

There's a life yet to be born

?

I

I stop to wonder why

And what is behind the "I"

Face that I came to recognize

Stories built on lies

Then the bartender brings my drink

And I pause my brain

And forget to think

Inner Voice

Among the nothingness I stand

Not a woman, not a man

Unidentifiable, as their definitions stand

Energy, yellow and red

Sparks flying out of my head

A strange creature

I become

I search for reasons to scream

I find none

Uninspired by this universe

The inner voice and I merge into one

The Speech

I am the universe disguised as a human

I am the seed turning into a tree

I am the stars that you cannot fathom

I am the idea you refused to believe

I am potential waiting to happen

And all things that proceed

I am your mother and your children

I am everything you see

Said the God within me

The Fall

I'm just a reflection of the thing possessing me

Of a soul entrapped in a tower without a key

Forgive it

It has forgotten what was and where it used to be

A god reduced to a human

Falling by choice just to see

The happiness after the sadness

And the naivety of thinking it's free

Moments

How can the end just begin

When I was just promised a tomorrow

That day that never comes

I spend my nights begging to borrow

Another minute or two

With people much like you

People who care

About little moments like these

The Stranger I Know

Naked

Like me

You were born

For them all to see

Naked

Screaming-- probably

Thinking why

Why must I cry

Air too painful

Consuming your lungs

...

See! We were the same once

Now, we are strangers on the street

Connection

After the sun has set

And the birds have vanished, to places I cannot see

I lay awake

Much too aware of my essence

That thing I try to avoid

That humanity that gives me much pain, and
sometimes pleasure

I see it

A fire that does not burn, nor is red

I see my soul trying to connect

But these webs are much too wide

And your humanity prevents you from admitting the
need

To be connected, once more

To be freed

Adam- Or So They Said

He asked for forgiveness

For crimes he's yet to commit

For the falling angels, and the apple they ate

He asked for the truth to be hid from children

For the story to be so grand

And they changed his name to Adam

And they clouded the truth behind the man

...

But he told me once-- In a dream I did not have

"The man was an angel that hid his wings." he laughed

"Under the apple tree." He pointed with smile so great

"The truth of the man was misspoken."

And what a false image did they paint

Live

He said he hated himself

Then he realized

The self he hates

And the self, doing the hating

Are separate entities

So, he killed what he loathed

Whilst living

Getting Older

The things you were dying for

Are the things you don't want anymore

Freedom

Wandering soul

Where do you wish to go?

Who of all

Told you, you can do so?

Freedom is for fools

So, you chose to be free

And cut these ties away from me

The Ant

The ant circled my empty plate, hopeful

He moved with purpose

But I

Sitting high

Can see the desert he is yet to discover

...

I wondered how I looked to God

Or a being much bigger than myself

Then I washed the ant away

And put the plate

Back on the shelf

.

Now

Because forever is a long, long time

She agreed to enjoy the moment

Lesson

He wished for me to lose the fight

He wished it for me despite what I was fighting for

And I hated him for it

Until I learned

Winning wasn't the lesson I needed to learn

My Spirit

I called to the spirit within

That thing that drives me

And forces me to begin

Another journey

Another day

Another hour

And here she stays

Not far

In fact, she's so close that I couldn't see

She was me

The Tree and Me

Not much difference between you and I

Branches bare

Extended to the sky

Feeling the leaves falling

Insanity calling

And our heads remaining high

We're not different, you and I

Our roots extended beyond our view

And we are judged by where we were planted

Not by what we do

We bear fruits that offend the palate of few

But oh, they don't know the healing we can brew

The Lesson I Did Not Learn

Welcome back, they said

As I was born

Eyes refusing to open

Mouth protesting existence

"Another life time to live?"

"Another lesson to learn?"

I have lived too many lives to count

Yet I am still being reborn

For a lesson I refused to learn

A Realization [Almost]

For a moment, much too short

I discovered the truth that can't be told

Then as I woke

It was all forgotten once more

Caterpillar

Don't cry

This pain is transformation

Part III

Of Magic and Madness

You might feel bad for a child born in a third world country. No toys or T.V. and worst of all, no candy! But Raghad loved making her own toys and creating her own stories. She dug in the mud until she found solid clay, and she created houses and toys out of it. She treasured the one can of Pepsi her mother brought home after a trip out of their village. She would freeze half of the can and enjoy it for days! Cucumber sandwiches and watermelon balls kept her cool on hot Iraq days. There, her imagination was cultivated, away from the distractions of television. This chapter is the fruit of her imagination and the hot summer days.

The Pond

A hesitant kiss on the cheek, close to her mouth.

He doesn't know what to do, can't stop the train.

Soon she'll be gone.

"The frogs in the pond!" he yelled "They are begging you to stay… it's not just me!"

"These trees! They cried all night while you laid between the sheets."

"And you know the cricket, that one that you asked me to take outside, he sung by our window all day long…it's not just me dear, it's not just me!"

She couldn't look him in the eye. One-way ticket is all she can afford. Is all she wanted-- secretly.

The vibrations of the ground told him that the train is near.

There's nothing he can do.

He looked at her, with a sad smile: "Look at me darling!"

"You know, the mountains won't meet the flat ground you're going to…the smell of hot concrete will make you miss the pond's stench. The stars!

They won't be visible dear! Won't you miss the stars?"

Her cold hands that he held on to, were so warm once.

She wasn't in love anymore. The pond was a thing of the past…she's ready for the next train.

She didn't even pack her cloths.

A hand bag is all she took, filled with papers and colored pens… and a dried old flower that he couldn't remember giving her.

She hasn't stopped loving him; she just needed a new muse.

Her fuel was inspiration and the pond has run out.

Colored Glasses

He knew what was wrong but could not be corrected

He looked at the mirror and hated what it reflected

Images no longer compelling

A stranger in the same old setting

He wanted to die just to start again

Then he slept and woke up a different man

Glasses with no prescription

Changed his perception

His eyes fooled him, you see

They kept him from being free

All he needed were colored glasses made by his
daughter

Saying happy new year to the world's best father

The Red Traffic Light

Look at this world of mine

There are lights and street signs

Detours and construction zones

Things I never thought I'd see

...

Strange how life turned out to be

From the thirty-minute walk in January cold

Just to get to a class and do as I'm told

...

To the wild dogs chasing after me

The rain following close behind

...

I never thought I would find

Myself complaining about a traffic light

Love

Brother, my chains are heavy

Sister, give them to me

Stand

They told me to start over

But I've only begun

They said to change my course

That I am not the one

Yet I stand

High above the ground

I stand, and I will not back down

Slow

A bare foot on a snow day

I want to feel this life I was given

Rain washing me away

I don't run

I stand still as I see it coming

I see them run

Rushing to avoid life

Hurrying to graves too expensive to buy

Burn me!

When did digging in dirt become a luxury?

Or carry me into the ocean

Set me free!

I will remember rain drops on my face

Cold snowy days

Earth I touched -- Earth that touched me

Please friends

Slow your journey

And don't be in a rush and a hurry

You

There's so much more to YOU

Than you know

Vague Memory

I often seek

Things I cannot find

Where are the fairies?

Why did we leave them behind?

They lived on my kitchen sink

I remember the songs they used to sing

There they stood

There

They might be standing, still

In a childhood home

A dream or reality

I cannot tell

...

My "wisdom" blocks the images I long to remember

Grandma's Chicken

"He is... He's like grandma's chicken."

Said the 6-year-old me when asked: "what is God?"

I explained how I saw grandma's chicken taking care of her eggs and the duck's eggs that looked drastically different. Then, she raised the ducklings as her own.

I saw kindness

I thought that was the definition of God

Dream

I dream of things that cannot be

Of angels and demons singing to me

Of life so easy

Worlds so bright

Of suns and stars shining through the night

And I wake

Trapped in this world of mine

Awaiting a magical sign

To finally define

Peace

The Magic

I stopped, once

To smell the roses

The bees protested my presence

So, I learned to admire the bees

And the work they do

There's magic beyond the colors that you see

There's even magic in the black and yellow bee!

Where?

I lost it

Somewhere

Between parking lots

Traffic lights

And

T.V. screens

That magic I used to see

Unaided

The Universe in My Hair

I found the magic

Hidden

Underneath a rock

I found the pieces

The Big Bang had left

Scattered in my hair

And I knew then

I was as old as this universe

And as young as I believed

I was just a piece

Of the many

...

And a hair that needs a wash

Simple Things

The vines gave way

As if they were welcoming me

And the trees danced with glee

The vibrations of the ground synchronized with my
own

And I knew then

I was home

The Lost Shoe

Am I so strange that I tend to see

Things that cannot be

An inspiring lost shoe

Turned into poetry

Who did it belong to

And how can its pair

Be made functional with this one laying here

?

The Bird's Secret

She wanted to fly

But the atmospheric pressure was too high

She wrapped herself in helium balloons

But the gas escaped them too soon

She wanted to fly

But her dreams were crushed by some physics guy

And her biology failed her at every try

She decided to transform

A bird in the sky, free to roam

So, the next time you see a bird fly

It might just be her, mocking that physics guy

The Voices

There is music in my head

Ringing old words, I have never read

Voices that say...

Something I can't make out

I try to shut them down, but I cannot

So, I let the madness consume me

As I become one

With the voices

And I know, they have won

As strange as it might sound

The voices pointed to where my sanity can be found

Piece

We were pieces

Broken apart

Thought to be insignificant

And through time we got lost

But when we come together

The image appears

And we finally realize that the bigger picture needs

Its missing piece

Fairies

They led me behind a broken barn

They showed me all the things they have done

Creatures that looked like smoke

They appeared and disappeared as they spoke

The river branch was their highway

The trees, their home

The forest under the mushrooms was their own

How did I come to such a world? I do not know

Among magical creatures that dance and glow

A world inside of my world that I have never seen

This taught me that things are never what they seem

Gypsy

Could you be lost

In a world where GPS is a click away?

Could you wander, with no destination as where to
stay?

A tent full of wonderful things

Light enough to carry

Little left for worry

Can I be lost with you?

I'm in need

To wander at your speed

The King

Maybe it was the lack of throne that made him
uneasy

He sat on an elevated chair

Screaming at his subjects

Feed me!

The king is a child, two-years-old

And the parents, must do as they're told

For the punishment is much too great

Nap time might get delayed!

New Paths

They say, there are no boundaries

At the bounds of imagination

But all they can see

Is the path already taken

They must have been mistaken

To think

The new path can be seen

From that movie screen

Maybe

They are too lazy

To make their own reality

Fool

Our dreams were so big

They thought us fools

Our path was so new

For their old tools

Yet we pave, a foot after another

And we create new dreams for others

To follow

For they think their dreams are too big to come true

Don't let that fool be you

.

Make Magic

Digging

Nails full of dirt

Trying to find a magic spell

That was lost

Losing my sanity

Despising gravity

Then

I remember!

I wrote the spell once before

I can write it once more!

Little Boat

I birthed it

The story that I wrote

Out of a dream I had

Of me sailing on a little boat

Soon I woke with vague memory

Thoughts I could not define

What was I doing on a boat in that dream of mine?

Lost and Found

Somehow

You forgot how to fly

You believed it was a childish lie

And you buried your wings apart from your heart

Now you're lost

Not sure where to start

Friend, dig deep below your brain

You'll find a treasure screaming out your name

Free the wings you used to have

And fly happily for the rest of your life

Little Child

I've searched for her

Time and time again

She chooses to hide

Underneath my skin

...

Eyes opened so wide

Searching for what's inside

Where have you gone

Little child?

Late

I get lost in lines they make

An illegal U-turn leading to a mistake

Between red and green light

While driving too slow at night

I get lost with a GPS that orders me around

Two streets away from your house

I walk in, trying not to make a sound

Late again

Much too late

"Where were you? Did you get lost again?"

I was watching the stars and got lost in my head

But I'm happy to find you, again, in our bed

Lost Scripts

The editing changed the meaning

Like Photoshop changed the girl

But this time no beauty was added

No

Not at all

And you lost the original

It's on a napkin on a floor

In a bar that you hardly remember

From the night before

The Child

She paints her mirror colors she wishes to see

The reflection finally shows what she wants to be

If you look through her glasses, you will understand

That your world is much too bland

Don't

Don't try to save her

She is singing in her head

Trapping the thoughts you had said

Turning them to something beautiful instead

Don't try to pull her away from the heaven that you
call hell

For you don't know in which hole that beauty fell

Missing Wings

She found it odd

That she could not fly

They told her she couldn't

But she didn't understand why

So, she jumped from the highest building she could find

She knew that her wings would never leave her behind

And then she knew

It did not take wings to fly

She believed it and so, she soared high

The Lost Things

Starving for inspiration

I dive into my imagination

Just to find pieces that I left behind

Like that stormy day that we found out

We had to move to a new place

A new country

A new space

Arriving, I felt my roots being ripped apart

Trees that over grew, beginning a new start

Starving for inspiration

I look for my imagination

That I can no longer find

Where's that secret world I created

The one behind my closet door?

Can you, please, help me find it once more?

My Madness

Without a passport, I travel

To lands of my own

To a world that does not require

A paper or a big loan

But you must bring a bit of madness

And love for fingers covered in paint

Hair so messy

And people who can appreciate

The madness within

Through Her Glasses

They made sure that her new glasses blocked the rays
she used to see

That the magic that distracted her as a child, can no
longer be

And so she saw the lights red, yellow and green

But she did not see the fairies behind the scene

She saw the clocks turning

The appointments that must be met

She no longer saw the creatures that helped

And as a 40-year-old woman

She remembered dreams she thought she had

Of a fairy she befriended

A troll she chased one night

"It must've been my imagination" she thought

Until she remembered to take off her adult glasses

Visions

The creatures crawled out of her book

And the painting stepped out of the frame

She knew that her imagination grew strong

But this time it did not feel the same

As if a veil has been lifted

She can finally see the creatures around

And with her new vision

She saw, there's much more to be found

Eyes Wide Open

Crawling out of the dark cave where I tend to hide

I hear noises

I see light

I force myself to open my eyes

I take it all in

I realize

Tree branches can dance

Creatures big and small put me in a trance

I gain my lost smile

I, once, loved this place

It's like a familiar face

I longed to remember

Someone I lost one cold December

But the leaves are turning green

And so, it seems that I must put the past behind

I can no longer choose to be blind

The Pond

Part 2

An unexpected visitor

The bird that sat on her window, it looked familiar as if it belonged to a different place

She can see that the city was not his home

Maybe he followed her train to where the trees don't grow

Where the cars' noises block the voices in her head

She can no longer hear her best friend— inspiration

Looking out of her cold studio apartment's window, she can't see the stars

Her lover's words resonate in her ears, he was right— she misses counting the bright pins in the sky

That yellow cheerful bird's singing covered all the other noises around her

She wondered if he had been a messenger, if he carried a letter from The Pond to her

Although her apartment stood high above the man-made trails beneath

It was no match to the mountain she used to live by

The broken kitchen counters that he'd promised to fix

The cotton filled pillows

The wooden chair he proudly carved

She closes her eyes humming with the bird,
harmonies she once knew so well

She can smell it, the pond's stench— what she hated
and loved so much

But it escapes her before she can capture it; she
wished to paint it on her pale grey wall

The memories grew old, and the paint has run dry

Morning Breeze

Smell of a morning breeze

Is all I need

Somedays

To sweep me back

To my old place

Home

Or so I called it

Is where fairies and elves

Gathered

To keep me safe

To ward off evil

To get me to this morning breeze

To days like these

I think of thanking them

Those things that got me here

But they long have disappeared

I still find them

Hidden between autumn leaves

On a morning breeze